For my husband Mac; our children, Harrison and Tawney; their spouses, Zach and Chaz; our grandchildren, Skylar and Owen; and one of my best friends, Beth Curry, whom I miss dearly every day.

www.mascotbooks.com

Let's Take a Hike: 7 Family-Friendly Trails on Nantucket

The information in this book is meant to supplement, not replace, proper hiking training. Like any sport involving speed, equipment, balance and environmental factors, hiking poses some inherent risk. The authors and publisher advise readers to take full responsibility for their safety and know their limits. Before practicing the skills described in this book, be sure that your equipment is well maintained, and do not take risks beyond your level of experience, aptitude, training, and comfort level.

For more information, please contact:
Mascot Books
620 Herndon Parkway #320
Herndon, VA 20170
info@mascotbooks.com

CPSIA Code: PRFRE0320A
Library of Congress Control Number: 2020901102
ISBN-13: 978-1-64543-332-3

Printed in Canada

Let's Take a Hike

7 Family-Friendly Trails on
Nantucket

Leslie Bains
Illustrated by Danny Moore

Table of Contents

History of Nantucket

Nantucket has a rich history: from a sleepy 17th century farming community to its reign as the whaling capital of the world in the 1700s and 1800s, to its recent incarnation as a flourishing art community and tourist destination. The island boasts some of the finest 18th and 19th century architecture in the nation. Its historic town was proclaimed a National Historic Landmark in 1966, and the designation extended to the entire island in 1971. Thanks to the stringent efforts of the Conservation Foundation and Land Bank, over half of its land has been conserved and remains undeveloped for visitors to enjoy.

Introduction

On every hike I take on Nantucket, there comes a stunningly simple moment that leaves its memory with me, like an osprey diving to catch a fish or a turtle in June laying its eggs. Sometimes it is just a moment that leaves me with a small smile. But there always comes a moment.

My eleven-year-old granddaughter and I were walking along Sconset Bluff one sunny day when we came across a seashell that someone else had clearly already found. It was painted with a question: "What does Cinderella wear to the beach?" On the opposite side was the answer: "A glass flipper."

My nine-year-old grandson from Los Angeles and I were hiking over the boardwalks of Stump Farm when we heard a strange noise that made him stop short and stand very still. "What is that noise?" he asked. I said, "That's a bullfrog." No bullfrogs walk the streets of Los Angeles.

My husband walked with me across the Coloured Cemetery near Mill Hill, stopping to read bits of American history etched into the headstones. They give a wonderful perspective about the people of color who arrived on this island in the 1700s and their struggle for freedom.

On the following pages are seven hikes that range in length from half a mile to 3 miles. Most average 1.5 to 2 miles. Modest descriptions of trees, flowers, birds, and other animals you might spot are included in each section.

In addition, I have included fun facts about each hike and also a couple of questions you can ask your children to engage their minds as well as their feet. There is a Latin phrase that says: *Solvitur Ambulando*. It means, "It is solved by walking." This small island, so many miles away from the mainland, is the perfect place to take a hike and see the wisdom of that ancient saying.

Whenever possible I will keep directions very simple. Rather than following north, south, east, and west, I tried to provide easy directions, such as "make a sharp right at the fork on the trail."

Enjoy these seven hikes around Nantucket!

Essentials to take on a hike:

1. *Water, water, and more water!*

2. *Hat*

3. *Sun protection*

4. *Decent shoes—a pair of sneakers are fine; no need to invest in hiking boots for these walks.*

5. *Bug or tick spray*

6. *A small day pack*

7. *A leash for your dog and bags to pick up after them. Nantucket has a leash regulation that is strictly enforced.*

Hike 1

Sconset Bluff, Erosion Project, and Sankaty Lighthouse

Location: Sconset is at the end of Milestone Road and can be reached by the bike path, by car, or by the NRTA bus system.

History: Sconset was settled as a fishing village in the 17th century. In 1877, Edward Underhill bought land in the village and rented small cottages to summer tourists. In 1881, a narrow gauge railway was built between Nantucket Town and Sconset Village. The railroad was originally on the south shore, but due to numerous washouts, it was moved to the middle of the island, which eventually became Milestone Road. The railroad never really made any money and went bankrupt in 1918.

In the 1840s, the United States government decided to erect a lighthouse that would be Sankaty Lighthouse since there were over 700 shipwrecks due to the shoals off the coast. There was a home at the base of the lighthouse to house the keeper and his family. The entire bluff suffered terrible erosion over many years, and the lighthouse was moved to its current location in 2007. Wooden benches mark where the original lighthouse stood.

Directions: The Sconset Bluff walk starts after the rotary and Sconset Market. Bear to your left and you will see a small road named Broadway. Walk on this road and make a quick right on Front Street. Follow Front Street to the end and curve to the left along a shell path past the small cottages on the left

and right. Near the end of the shell path, you will see two grey pipes about four feet high. Take a right, then follow around to the left, and you will eventually see a marker on the grass labeled Public Way, which is the official start of the walk.

Stay on the Public Way as you pass the homes on your left. The dedicated homeowners maintain, in part, this walk so everyone can enjoy the magnificent views and flowers. Many of the staircases leading to the beach are private, but some are public. Either walk down the public stairs or sit down and take in the view. The beaches here are almost deserted.

Do NOT bring your dog as the Bluff is a place for strolling, not walking your dog. Sadly, erosion has cut off the last half mile to Sankaty Head Lighthouse. However, if you walk down Baxter Road toward Sankaty Lighthouse, you can see the Erosion Project experiment to save the bluff. Over the past twenty plus years, the bluff has been eroding at a rate of at least three feet per year. A number of homes have needed to be moved farther back on their property or even across Baxter Road.

Questions for Children:

What is a cistern? You can see one at Sankaty Lighthouse.

How did Sconset get its name?

What is a geotube?

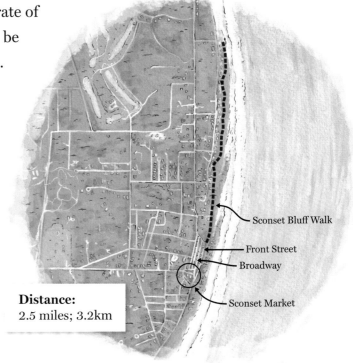

Sconset Bluff Walk

Front Street

Broadway

Sconset Market

Distance:
2.5 miles; 3.2km

6

Hike 2

Nantucket Field Station

Location: The University of Massachusetts Field Station is located on Polpis Road right after the Lifesaving Museum on the left. Turn in at #180 and park in the Visitors Parking area.

History: There are 110 acres spread over the harbor beach front, freshwater pond, salt marsh, and tidal flat that provide habitats for the feeding and breeding of many wildlife species. The Conservation Foundation purchased the property in 2004, but the University of Massachusetts continues to use the facilities for research.

Directions: After parking, walk through the wooden gate to your left and bear to the right. You can pick up a map of the property at the sign board to the right of the parking lot to see all the trails. The trail begins right after the wooden gate on a grassy mowed path. Follow the path up and down small hills. A variety of trees and shrubs grow here, including the Beach Pea, Marsh Mallow, Sweet Pepper Bush, Dusty Miller, and Bayberry. Keep an eye out for small deer paths through the bushes as well. Continue to the right until you arrive at Osprey Point.

The osprey platform is no longer there, but you can still enjoy the view from the bench of Polpis Harbor and Coatue. Walk along the grassy path here—do not walk along the fragile sand dune area. Continue along the bluff and then bear to the right. You should now be overlooking Folgers Marsh. Many birds live here, including the statuesque white egret. Because of the tides, salt marshes like this are among the most productive ecosystems on Earth.

Bear to the left and you will soon pass by the Field Station and surrounding buildings, including its laboratory. Continue on the car path a short distance until you come to a small grassy path on the right. Take it and you will see more of Folgers Marsh and a single tree surrounded by a circle of grass. Legend has it, if children walk around this "wishing tree" three times and make a wish, it will come true.

Questions for Children:

What is an osprey, and how many osprey nests are there on Nantucket?

What is an egret?

What is Coatue?

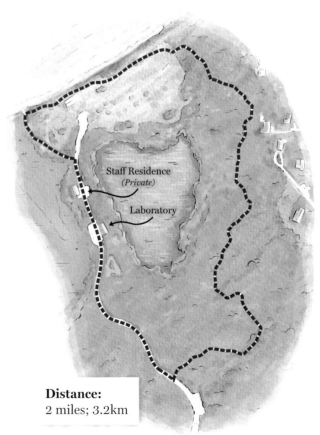

Staff Residence
(Private)

Laboratory

Distance:
2 miles; 3.2km

Hike 3

Stump Pond Trail and the Nantucket Shipwreck & Lifesaving Museum

Location: Take the Polpis Road for about 4.5 miles heading toward Sconset. The trail is off Almanack Pond Road, past the Nantucket Lifesaving Museum on your left and the house mailbox #278 on your left. Turn right onto Almanack Pond Road, and just past the Almanack Arts Colony on your right is a small dirt parking area named the Norwood Farm parking lot.

Park your car or bike in the lot and cross the dirt road. The trail is marked to your left by a small stake with a white blaze. This is Stump Pond Trail.

History: During the 19th century, bad weather and treacherous shoals led to over 700 shipwrecks in the waters surrounding Nantucket. The Nantucket Shipwreck & Lifesaving Museum contains over 5,000 artifacts of shipwrecks and life-saving equipment. The Museum is open from late May through mid-October, Monday to Saturday from 10 a.m. to 5 p.m. and Sundays from noon to 5 p.m.

Directions: Stump Pond Trail is maintained by the Nantucket Land Bank with small wooden boardwalks across streams that swell up during heavy rains. Follow this trail through the forest with many scrub oaks, tupelo, red maples, and ferns. After crossing a couple of boardwalks, you will come to a Y. Take the little trail to the left and go down to the pond where you can find many birds, bullfrogs, and occasionally a white egret. Follow the trail next to the pond for a short while and then head up a little hill to rejoin the original trail. Continue on until you come to a slightly open area.

If you bear left up the hill, you will see a good portion of Stump Pond in the distance. Stump Pond is a man-made pond that was dug by men from Cape Verde to provide water to the cranberry bogs. When you are ready to leave, turn and go back down to the open area. If you go straight across, you will see a four-foot post. Bear right and go down a small, steep hill that will lead you to the Almanack Pond dirt car road with Almanack Pond straight ahead. Almanack Pond is a kettle pond, meaning it was formed during the glacial age thousands of years ago. Depending on the season, you may see sage grass or trees growing in the pond. This is also a nesting place for turtles, who lay their eggs on the side of the pond or road in June, so be cautious around the pond. If you see a snapping turtle, keep your distance—they are quite protective and can easily snap off a finger.

Questions for Children:

What are the 3 most common turtles on Nantucket?

What are the white birds you often see in the marshes in Stump Pond?

What is the name of the bird with the red wings?

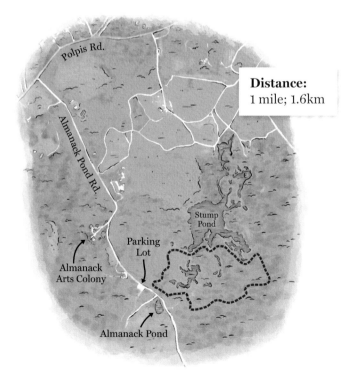

Distance: 1 mile; 1.6km

Hike 4

Mill Hill, Historic Cemetery, the Old Mill, and African Meeting House

Location: There are four small hills called Popsquatchet close to town. Head down Orange Street from Main Street and turn right on East York Street to reach Mill Hill. Cross Pleasant Street and continue up West York Street. The Old Mill will be on your right at the top of the hill, and a white sign across the street will say Historic Cemetery. If you are driving, there is a five-space parking area off Prospect Street beyond the Cottage Hospital at the turn-in for Historic Cemetery.

History: There is evidence of a small, black community on the island as early as 1710. Most were brought here as slaves. The Quakers were the first to begin emancipating them, and in 1805 the Proprietors voted to set aside one acre of land as a burial place. By the peak of the whaling period in 1840, there were 576 people of color living on the island, primarily working on the whaling ships. In 2008, the Selectman of Nantucket officially designated the cemetery at Mill Hill with the stakeholders' approval as the Coloured Cemetery. There are about 120 markers in the cemetery.

The Old Mill is the only remaining grist mill of the original five windmills on the island. It was built by Nathan Wilbur in 1746. Originally it was a post mill, which means the wheel and post could rotate the vanes depending on the direction of the wind. It is open from late May to mid-October from 11 a.m. to 4 p.m.

Directions: From the Historic Cemetery parking area, you will see three roads. The middle overlooks a grassy ravine down a small hill. Bear to the left of a sign on the dirt car road that says "Cemetery" and follow the narrow dirt hiking trail to a picnic table to your left and two park benches straight ahead.

Right before the benches, you will see a small trail marked by a stake with a white blaze. Follow this trail to a large old tree in a grassy area. Continue straight ahead into a larger grassy area where you may be able to see the vanes of the Old Mill to your left through the trees. Continue following the stakes with white blazes somewhat straight ahead until you see a split rail fence and the hospital helicopter landing pad. Cross the dirt path onto a grassy path through some brush, which will curve to the left up to the dirt road by the Coloured Cemetery.

After touring the cemetery, take the dirt car road to the left. It will veer off to the right up a hill where you will see two narrow trails. Take the grassy one almost straight ahead that goes along the back half of the grassy ravine. When the ravine appears, walk about 40 yards and take a trail up a small hill that's marked by a stake with a white blaze. As the trail weaves around, you should see a tree in a circle of grass. Bear right, and you will find a bench to commemorate Nantucketer Richard Walsh. The plaque reads, "Richard Walsh and his dog walked these paths and loved this valley in all seasons."

Make your way back to the parking lot. You can either take the steep, wide, dirt hill straight ahead from the bench down into the ravine and up again, or the path to the left of the bench that curves around. You can then walk up the ravine and across Prospect Street. Either way, you should be back at the Old Mill.

Highly recommended is a visit one block down West York Street to the African Meeting House. This was built in the 1820s as a schoolhouse and functioned as such until 1846 when Nantucket's schools were integrated. A complete restoration of the Meeting House and its surrounding wooden structures is underway. It is open year-round, but check their website for days and times.

Questions for Children:

What is the oldest marker in the cemetery?

What is the newest marker in the cemetery?

Who was Frederick Douglass, and how many times did he visit Nantucket?

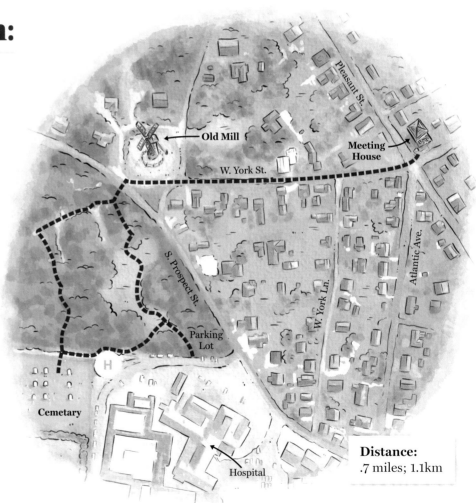

Distance:
.7 miles; 1.1km

Hike 5
Tupancy Links

Location: Tupancy Links is located off Cliff Road and can be reached by the Cliff Road biking path or from a small parking lot for about eight cars. This hike presents one of the most dramatic views of the Nantucket Sound. On a clear day, you can see the entrance to Nantucket Harbor, Coatue, and the Great Point Lighthouse, which is 8 miles away. You can also see Jetties Beach, the church steeples in town, the clock tower on top of the Unitarian Church, and Tuckernuck Island.

The Tupancy property is well maintained by the Nantucket Conservation Foundation. Many people walk their dogs or view a sunrise or sunset here. The grasslands are a wonderful place to fly kites as well.

History: Tupancy Links was originally part of the Nantucket Golf Course, which was established in 1921. It was a nine-hole course that was mowed by 200 sheep and 50 Angora goats. Mr. Oswald Tupancy bought the property in 1949 and operated it as a golf course for only a few years before he and his wife Sally decided to donate the property to the Conservation Foundation. The property is home to expansive grasslands, stands of pitch pine trees and Japanese black pine trees, blue stem grass, and many other species of wildflowers and grasses. It can also be home to poison ivy, so be sure to walk carefully and stay on the trail.

Directions: Enter Tupancy Links through the wooden post and take the trail to the left. Keep an eye out for white-tailed deer in the stand of trees to the right. Following along the trail, you will see another mowed grass footpath to the left up a small rise. At the top is a bench where you can view much of the former golf course. Take the small grassy path back to the original gravel trail, then turn left and follow around. As you bear to the right, you will come to a dirt path on the left in the shape of a T. Take this path to the bluff overlooking Nantucket Sound. To return, head back on the same path and make a left at the T, which will curve around and take you back to the parking lot. You will pass grasslands with Conservation Foundation markers. This is a great place to fly your kite if you've brought one!

Questions for Children:

How many lighthouses are on Nantucket, and where are they located?

What is the difference between a pitch pine and Japanese pine tree?

How many deer are on the island?

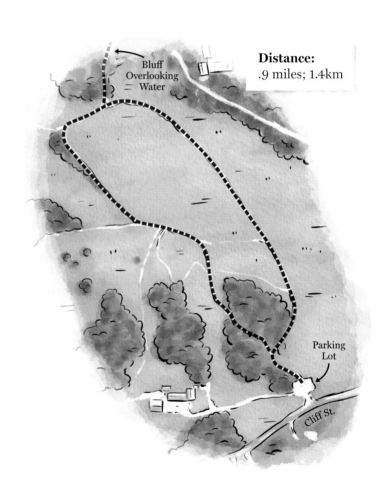

Distance:
.9 miles; 1.4km

Bluff Overlooking Water

Parking Lot

Cliff St.

Hike 6

Gardner Farm and Cisco Brewery

Location: Take Hummock Pond Road past the turn-off for Bartlett Farm on the left. Continue past the 167 Fish Market on your right. You can either drive or take the Cisco Bike Path. There is an open dirt parking area at the trail start for about 10 cars.

History: The Land Bank purchased the 41-acre parcel from the Gardner family in 1995. The land was farmed in the 1800s and 1900s. The area has many trails, and one leads to the edge of Hummock Pond, the largest pond in Nantucket.

Directions: Follow the dirt path between the split rail fence and then bear to the right onto a path with many pine trees. When the trail splits in the forest, bear left and continue straight. The path will dead end, so continue to the left and left again at the next fork. You will come to an open grassy field. Bear left and a small path will be at a 90-degree angle on your right, marked by a stake with a white blaze. Follow this down to Hummock Pond. Keep an eye out for Canadian geese and mute swans gliding past the phragmites (tall reeds) or turtle heads popping up in the pond.

Return to the grassy trail and bear right as you walk somewhat in a semi-circle. Keep the split rail fence to your right, and you will soon see a small trail to your right. Take this, and when the split in the path occurs, bear left. Cross over the boardwalk between the phragmites. Go up a small sandy hill, and you will see the houses along Hummock Pond Road. Continue bearing left until you reach the parking lot.

From the parking lot, cross over Hummock Pond Road and head to Cisco Brewery. This is a happening place with beer, wine, live music, and food trucks. Children are welcome.

Cisco Brewery opened in 1995 and is the sole brewer on the island. Hours are 11 a.m. to 7 p.m.

Questions for children:

What is a mute swan?

What are phragmites?

*How many major
ponds are on Nantucket?*

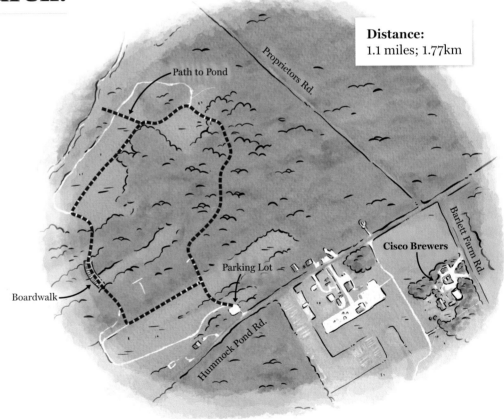

Distance:
1.1 miles; 1.77km

Proprietors Rd.

Path to Pond

Bartlett Farm Rd.

Cisco Brewers

Parking Lot

Boardwalk

Hummock Pond Rd.

Hike 7

Sanford Farm

Location: The entrance is off the Madaket Road in a large parking lot on the left, about 1.5 miles from town. There are three hikes on the property: one is 1.7 miles to the head of Hummock Pond, one is a 6 mile roundtrip to the beach, and the one covered here is 3.1 miles to the barn and back. Morning or late afternoon is the best time, as it can get fairly hot and there is little shade.

History: Sanford Farm, Ram Pasture, and the Woods covers 984 acres and was used during the 17th and 18th centuries for grazing sheep and cows, farming, and harvesting wood. It was an operating dairy farm until the early 1920s, and the barn is still standing.

Directions: Follow the informational markers from the parking lot to the barn. The path varies from dirt car tracks to grass and smaller dirt trails. On a clear day, you can see Hummock Pond and most of the south shore from Cisco to Madaket beaches.

Questions for Children:

How many different kinds of butterflies can you spot?

On the way back from the barn, see if you can spot a large orange/red sculpture in the distance. Who is the artist?

When did Hummock Pond divide into two ponds?

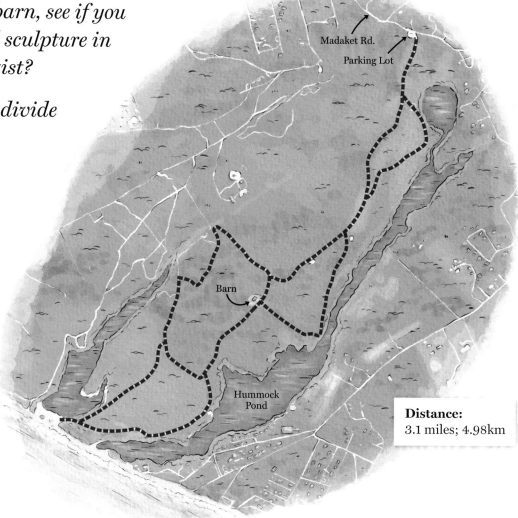

Madaket Rd.

Parking Lot

Barn

Hummock
Pond

Distance:
3.1 miles; 4.98km

Answers to Questions

Hike 1

1. A cistern is a tank used for storing water. They are usually built to collect rainwater. Cisterns were first used by the Greeks and the Romans thousands of years ago. They are still used today for farm irrigation.

2. There are 4 spellings: 'Sconset, Sconset, Siasconsett, and Sweseckech. It is derived from an a Native American word meaning "near the great whale bone."

3. A geotube is a long, durable plastic mesh filled with sand. It primarily helps to prevent erosion damage to shorelines.

Hike 2

1. There are more than thirty osprey nesting platforms. Ospreys, also known as fish hawks, make a long journey from Central and South

America to nest in Nantucket for the summer. They lay two to four eggs, and both the male and female take care of their young by sitting on the nest, feeding them, and teaching them to fly and fish for themselves.

2. An egret is a white heron that can be as tall as three feet and three inches. It has a yellow bill and black legs and feet. It usually feeds in shallow water on fish, frogs, and insects.

3. Coatue is 390 acres of barrier beach that shelters Nantucket from the waters of the sound.

Hike 3

1. There are three common turtles on Nantucket. The Eastern spotted turtle is the most common. It has bright yellow stripes behind its eyes and red/orange markings on the edge of its shell. Snapping turtles are the largest and have big jaws. There is also the spotted turtle, which has yellow and orange spots on its shell.

2. *There are six types of snakes on Nantucket, none of which are poisonous. The garter snake, which comes in many colors; the ring-necked snake, which has an orange underside; the Eastern milk snake, which has brown rings; the Northern water snake, which is grey or beige; the ribbon snake, and the smooth green snake.*

3. *This bird is called the red-winged blackbird. It also has a touch of yellow on its wings. The female is a dull brown. They migrate here from Mexico.*

Hike 4

1. *1812 Eliza Ann Williams. Back row to the right.*

2. *1957 Florence Voisinger. Near the metal railings.*

3. *Frederick Douglass was an abolitionist, writer, and orator. The wife of his slave owner in Maryland taught him to read and write. He escaped to the North and became a national leader for the abolitionist movement. Douglass spoke four times on Nantucket.*

Hike 5

1. *There are three lighthouses on Nantucket. Sankaty (see Hike #1 for details), built in the 1840s; Brant Point, located near town, built in 1746; and Great Point, located at the tip of Nantucket on the Coatue Wildlife Refuge, built in 1784.*

2. *Pitch pines are very hardy, and their branches are usually twisted. Their lifespan is usually 200 years, and their needles grow in bundles of three. The Japanese pine has a hard life on Nantucket due to a beetle invasion that kills them. Their needles grow in bundles of two.*

3. *There are about 2,500 to 4,000 deer on the island. Every year about 300 are killed during hunting season. Ticks live on the increasing deer population and are a danger to humans. Always check for ticks, a small, black insect, after a hike. If bitten, a simple blood test will determine if you have Lyme disease, which is easily treatable.*

Hike 6

1. *A mute swan has an orange bill and a long neck curved in an S shape. They eat about eight pounds of vegetation a day.*

2. *Phragmites are an invasive reed that borders most Nantucket ponds. Many birds breed in the phragmites to protect their young.*

3. *There are many ponds on Nantucket, but seven are considered Great Ponds, meaning they are over 10 acres in size.*

Hike 7

1. *Be sure to look for the orange Monarch, which migrates here from Mexico during the summer. The yellow and black swallowtail, the Eastern Tailed blue, the black and dark blue swallowtail, and the simple white moth are the most prevalent species.*

2. *The sculptor is Mark di Suvero. He was born in Shanghai, China, in 1933 and immigrated to San Francisco with his family in 1941. A graduate of the University of California, Berkeley, he received the National Medal of Arts in 2011 from President Obama.*

3. *Prior to 1978, Hummock Pond was shaped like a fish hook. During a fierce blizzard and nor'easter in 1978, the storm hacked off part of the pond known as Clark's Cove to create a separate pond.*

Acknowledgments

I want to thank my hiking buddies, Elaine Schwartz and Mary Bowler-Seidel, who kept up our rigorous pace even in the heat of the day. My husband put on his sneakers and hiked every trail with me without complaint, sometimes twice, offering his advice and more importantly his sense of humor. Our daughter Tawney read several drafts of sections, offering suggestions, plus taking a two-hour experimental hike with me that we collectively decided, "Not right for the book." Our son Harrison offered lots of support with many phone calls from California asking, "How is it going?"

My friend Jane Heller read the entire draft, asked many questions, and gave it her seal of approval. Also, my neighbors Lauri Altman Posner and Linda and Robert Williams encouraged me over the summer.

Allen Reinhard, senior ranger on Nantucket, provided a number of insights and background information on a number of hikes on Conservation Land. Dick Burns at Mitchell's Bookstore on Main Street provided excellent suggestions on the focus of the book. Most of all, a special thanks to John Stanton, filmmaker and journalist at the *Nantucket Inquirer and Mirror* who provided his excellent editing skills, refocusing my narrative in a couple of sections.

About the Author

Leslie E. Bains has been a resident and visitor to Nantucket since the late 1970s. She was President of the Nantucket Theater Workshop and is on the Board of the Nantucket Lighthouse School. Leslie had a distinguished forty plus year career in private banking and investments and was the highest-ranking woman as Senior Executive Vice President of HSBC. She was also president of AFS International, the largest student exchange program in the world with offices in fifty countries.

Throughout her career, Leslie has been involved as a corporate director and trustee of many companies and nonprofits.